I0511217

EXPERIMENTAL VENTRILOQUISM

DIANA ROCKWELL

Foreword By Tom Ladshaw

Cover Design by Diana Rockwell and Co.

Edited by Tom Ladshaw

Copyright © 2016 Diana Rockwell

All rights reserved.

ISBN-10:1539639665
ISBN-13:978-1539639664

CONTENTS

DISCLAIMER

This book is **not** a how-to/ step-by-step guide on learning ventriloquism basics. In fact, it is not recommended to read this before learning and understanding the technique of ventriloquism. This book is written for those already pursuing the art and who are seeking new and original methods to consider.

The purpose of this book is to familiarize ventriloquists with a variety of principles in fine art and incorporating them into their performances. These methods are <u>**not**</u> guaranteed to work for everybody, but they have helped me over the years and I wish to share them with you. Enjoy!

-Rockwell

FOREWORD

In 1945, psychologist Karl Duncker proposed a fascinating problem. He offered subjects a box, some thumbtacks, a candle and some matches, with the instructions to his subjects to use the items at hand to attach the candle to the wall. Some tried to melt the candle to the wall. Some tried to use tacks to attach the candle to the wall. Very few came up with the actual solution, which was to use the tacks to attach the box itself to the wall, then place the candle inside it. And thus, the phrase "thinking outside the box" was born.

In this fascinating new work, ventriloquist Diana Rockwell proves that "thinking outside the box" can be a legitimate technique, not just a goal to strive for. Using her background in fine art, Diana explains several new techniques with which a ventriloquist can create not only material for existing characters, but entirely new characters as well!

Our work as ventriloquists includes not just the nuts-and-bolts of speaking without moving the lips and operating a puppet, but the actual creation of the character for the puppet and the material it will use. I've always been a firm believer in embracing new technologies and new techniques to enhance our work. The use of the ideas and techniques revealed herein will enable you to think in different ways and add originality and creativity to your own work.

Read this volume with an open mind. It will be new and foreign to you at the beginning. But as you begin to understand and become more comfortable with the ideas presented to you, you will discover entirely new presentational ideas, character concepts, and even actual jokes. This type of book is rare (if not unique) in the canon of ventriloquial works: It charts an entirely new course of original, creative thinking for those progressive enough to try it.

Read it. Think about it. Read it again. Then try it. I honestly believe you'll be surprised and delighted with the new creative vistas that open up to you.

-- Tom Ladshaw

INTRODUCTION

When I was an undergrad, I started out at a community college as a painting major. I discovered my love for ventriloquism when I enrolled in my second year at KU. It began when I watched an episode of *Identity* hosted by Penn Gillette. This was a show that had a group of people standing on stage and the contestant had to identify their titles from a list based solely on physical appearances. In one episode, Bruce Jenner (pre Caitlyn) made an appearance as one of the people to identify. He wore a black tuxedo and bow tie. The contestant had immediately mistaken him for being a ventriloquist! This moment was a turning point for me because it was the first time since the fourth grade that I had even heard the word "ventriloquist."

My first exposure to a ventriloquist happened when I was in the fourth grade and one appeared at our school for an assembly about being drug-free. I don't remember the his name, but the performance was pure golden. He was not at all like most of vents I've seen perform nowadays. In one act, he performed with a figure of a young girl that had removable body parts, including the top of her head so that we could see her brain. It was creepy to

all of us, yet I didn't want this assembly to stop. Everyone I knew liked it.

My next-door neighbors and I had talked about it for quite some time. That

was also the same year I became a fan of The Goosebumps book *Night of*

The Living Dummy. Millennial vents, like myself, are what I like to refer to

as growing up in the "Slappy Age" of ventriloquism. Ventriloquists from

previous generations either owned a Charlie McCarthy doll or a Danny

O'Day doll at some point. Millennial vents either owned a copy of that book,

or owned a Slappy doll. He was our Charlie. With that flashback, I was

immediately reminded of what I was put on God's green earth to do.

Since that turning point, I was inspired by countless YouTube videos of

ventriloquists performing. It started with Kevin Johnson's audition for

America's Got Talent (please watch if you've never seen it, you'll be blown

away) and eventually I fell in love with the works of Dan Horn (my fave). A

small part of me was wanting to continue with visual arts, but painting

wasn't getting me anywhere. I was okay at it, but I was nowhere

near as good as I needed to be in order to get by. Majoring in fine art is rewarding, but it comes with a serious downside: attempting to innovate when everything imaginable had already been done, or so it seemed. This is where the phrase "art is dead" comes in. I got to the point to where I just didn't like it anymore and needed to embrace what I couldn't stop thinking about. As I taught myself ventriloquism, I purchased Edgar Bergen's book *How To Become A Ventriloquist* and Kolby King's *Ventriloquism Made Easy.* Both are absolutely excellent reads for beginners.

I finished both books quickly and then I purchased *Dumbstruck* by Stephen Connor. Now that one was a difficult read, but it showed me that ventriloquism did in fact have an intellectual side. In this book, he includes topics such as The Oracle of Delphi, The Witch of Endor from The Book of Samuel, telekinesis, the invention of the telephone, and of course, media which featured ventriloquism. One book that I discovered upon reading that book was *The Indiscreet Jewels* by Denis Diderot. It is an allegory about The Sultan of Congo and how he could make a woman's genitals talk by using a magic ring. Not exactly G-rated, but it is an interesting read.

Eventually, I bought my first puppet: a little red heart from eBay that I named Ira. To quote what one of my art instructors once said "If you can't make it good, make it big. It you can't make it big, make it red." Ira was a bright cherry popsicle red *and* he is now bigger than he once was. I always wanted to make him big, good *and* red. The character that immediately came to mind was a smart ass with sarcastic comments to everything. I eventually added devil horns and a devil tail. I even threw in this joke: you can't spell 'irate' without 'Ira.'

I started out by taking him with me to open mic poetry nights at a college hangout called The Jazzhaus. The first Wednesday of each month was dedicated to poetry. My first few times around went great, others were just okay, and sometimes the audience was completely dead. My favorite thing to use Ira and poetry for was looking up random poems on Google written by crybaby emo kids. But if the ones we found weren't funny enough, then my roommate and I would make up our own. I would then tell my audience it was found on Myspace (what the audience doesn't know won't hurt them). Having Ira react to the silliness and self-pitying of the poem (or 'emoem' as I call them) was a hit with the crowd. It was the type of humor they could relate to.

I took a poem writing class as an English credit and the idea of preparing bad poetry was when we were asked to write intentionally bad poems. Mine immediately got a laugh from everyone in the class when I opened with this line: *Dear diary, life is so unfair…*

This same poetry class was where I learned the *Questions And Answers* or *If And Then* games as seen in the Dada section of this book and it's how I came up with silly ideas for bad poems to share. I had never seen another vent tell 'emo' jokes before and I only did it temporarily because the 'emo' trend was becoming dated.

I eventually recorded videos of myself as a plan to post on YouTube called "Rockwell's Bottom 5's" and it was a show dedicated to "worst of" categories. I decided not to post them online because I wasn't interested in posting videos that could stir up hatred (especially if I eventually wanted to perform family friendly shows). Not to mention, a lot of these videos contained borrowed music, which is a violation of intellectual property risking that my videos could be taken down, so I just made these to share with my friends. Some of these categories included worst tattoos, worst lyrics, worst songs from the 90's, and dumbest quotes from pop stars. They were a ton of fun to make, but I have zero regrets about not posting them online.

In my painting courses, one of my instructors gave me the best advice I have ever been given about anything artistically: avoid the obvious. That has always been my mission with ventriloquism and it always will be. I make certain there are memorable experiences for people in every show I do, even school assemblies. I was fortunate enough to perform an assembly about being drug-free at the same school I saw once saw it at. It was so rewarding to know that I could go up on stage and enable the same experience for children of this generation.

In that assembly, I took a risk and physically tossed my puppet into the audience. Kids were shocked, but they immediately burst into laughter. And of course, they were sweet enough to hand him back. I also included an interactive segment where I would have students come up on stage and show my puppet and I what they learned. I also included workbooks that I

designed myself for them to color and take home. That same school asked

me to come back. I've now performed there at least seven or eight times and

the kids remember me each year. One thing I was asked to do was put

together a presentation about ventriloquism for their career day fair. I never

really considered myself very successful, financially, but it sure felt great to

share the same podium as doctors, lawyers, public authorities, and even a

cage fighter.

I attended the Vent Haven convention for the first time in 2014. I fell in

love with the community right away and never wanted to leave. I have been

attending each year from then on out and plan to keep it that way. In 2015, I

was a finalist for Lee's Summit's Got Talent which represented talent acts of

the greater Kansas City area. That same year I was awarded the Clinton

Detweiler scholarship presented by Terry Fator. I submitted a video of

myself and my character, Zander. We combined ventriloquism with fast pace

hip hop music (yes, America's Got Talent has contacted me).

I've come up with several ideas over the years for innovative vent acts, *x.*

but in order for ventriloquism to reach it's peak, it mustn't be done

by a single person. It must be done by several persons. That is why I am

passing my artistic knowledge on to you, the ventriloquist reading this book.

You are reading this for a reason. You know as well as I do that you can

make a difference with one of the most remarkable skills on the planet.

Being a highly skilled ventriloquist takes a lot of time, effort, and discipline.

The illusion of it is awe inspiring to others. They want to see an expert. If

they notice poor lip control, they *will* point it out. Don't half ass the

technical side of things, but be creative in your endeavors.

And yes, being funny is a big part of being a ventriloquist. However, it's

not the *only* part. Why not make your audience laugh *and* give them an

experience that they will never ever forget? I would say the same thing to a

musician or a writer. Sure, a catchy song or a fun story is great, but make it

stand apart from the others. Have a signature style. Señor Wences had a

signature style, more so than any vent I have ever seen. I'm not at all saying

"be like Señor Wences," I'm saying be *you* and be the best possible you.

I open this book with a statement as made seen the disclaimer: the ideas I've written out aren't guaranteed to work for everybody, but you will never know until you *experiment*.

ART HISTORY

In this section I am going to briefly evaluate movements in art history that attribute to what it means to think outside the box: Abstract Expressionism, Dadaism, Minimalism, and Pop Art. If there was one lesson I was taught as an undergrad that applies to all art forms it is this: avoid the obvious. By saying that to myself over and over again, it had me thinking: what makes a work of art predictable? This is the time to sit back and make an inventory in your head of concepts that have been overdone. One that I am particularly sick of is this dialogue from multiple romance movies: "Look me in the eye, tell me you don't love me."

"I don't love you."

"You just lied."

Of course, that is just one example of overused movie dialogue. By pinpointing this, we are recognizing a cliche. Now use this same tactic to find cliches in ventriloquism. I have provided space for you to make notes on the following page:

NOTES

_____

_____

_____

_____

_____

_____

_____

_____

_____

_____

_____

_____

Once you've had the time to think that through, we can move onto the next step: using principles from fine art movements and applying them to ventriloquism. These are listed alphabetically.

ABSTRACT EXPRESSIONISM: This art movement was prevalent in the 1940's and 1950's, most notably in New York. These artists were not only known for using large scale canvases filled with dominant colors (also known as *color field* painting), but a lot of them also incorporated highly expressive brushstrokes and painterly gestures. The key visual element of these works is *raw emotion*. In a color field painting, the emotional impact is more subtle and limited on colors and textures (Mark Rothko is a perfect example of this). In the more expressive style, the emotional impact is aggressive and loaded with a chaotic assortment of colors (Willem de Kooning is an example of this).

Now if Abstract Expressionism had an impact on ventriloquism, these would be the things to look for: **raw emotion**, **large scale**, and great profound **expression**.

"Raw emotion" can vary in multiple ways: it can play as a climactic point within your act (i.e. the extensive crying led to this point) and it can also

help create "reactionary humor." Overreacting of your character alone can

gain huge laughs, if used in the right context.

"Large Scale" can take place not just with the size of your figure, but

also the size of your stage space. This could be a chance for you to break

down your invisible fourth wall and interact with your audience in ways you

never thought imaginable.

What does it take to make an act "expressive?" It can be a facial

expression or bodily, not just from the figure; but also from the ventriloquist.

A joke can be written based on expression alone, with no intended

punchline.

DADAISM: This was a European avant-garde movement from the early

20th century that spread out to Berlin. Artists of this movement were

recognized as nihilistic because their focus was to break down the barriers of

traditional fine art. Dadaism is a term not only used in painting and

sculpture, but can also be applied to literary works and performance.

Ventriloquism is an art that does have a lot of barriers. On average, you'll hear people say that ventriloquists are "only supposed to be funny." Humor is a great thing. I care very much about making my audience laugh, but it is not my only goal. What I care about even more is giving them an experience like no other.

The way I see it, the average ventriloquist performs as if he is stuck in a small box. Now this is relating to what I previously stated about breaking down the fourth wall. The small box [the ventriloquist standing position] is trapped in a larger box [the stage]. While the theatre stage has four walls, the ventriloquist stage has eight. Why not break down each and every one of them? What I have done in my shows is physically throw my puppet into the audience. I save this for smaller crowds only so that I can easily spot my puppet. The "wall breaking" is one way to look at breaking tradition.

Another way to look at it is to think of other art forms that ventriloquism has not yet been combined with. Ventriloquism, like all art forms, is malleable. It can be mixed, matched, and remolded with anything you like. We are already familiar with combining it with stand up comedy. But why not take it a step further? Maybe somewhere in the world there could be a ventriloquist fronted rock band, or a ventriloquist ballerina, or a

Shakespearean ventriloquist (we can call this a soliloquist).

As I mentioned, Dadaism plays a role in writing as well as actions. What

I am going to share with you are a couple of literary games that can help

incorporate a different kind of humor into your act. Starting with: Dada

Poems.

Dada Poems can be written by cutting out lots of random words from

magazine clippings and placing them in a hat. Draw one word at a time and

glue it onto a sheet of paper in the order from which they were drawn. On

the next few pages, I have included a few examples of ones that I made

myself:

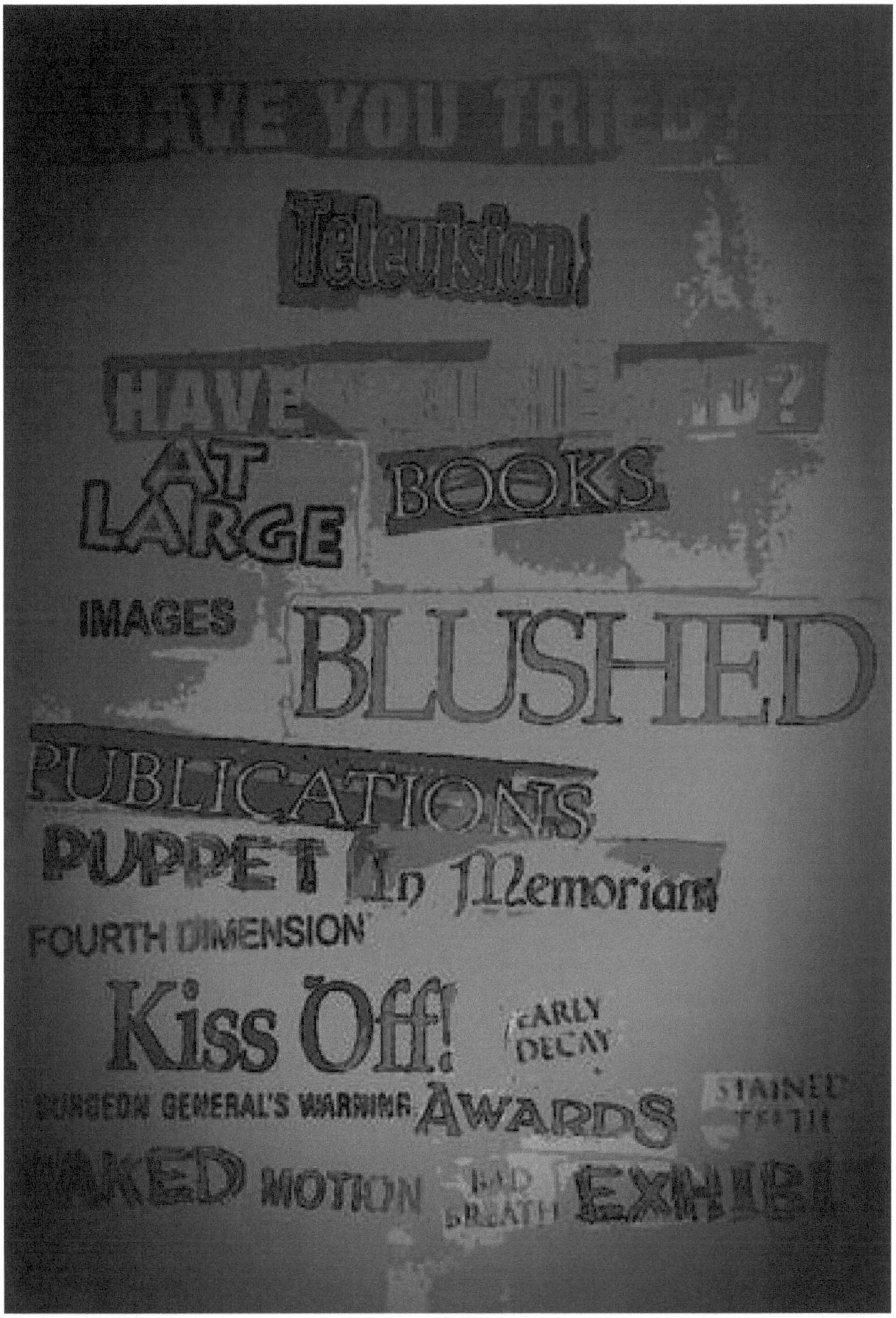
Television
HAVE
AT LARGE
BOOKS
IMAGES
BLUSHED
PUBLICATIONS
PUPPET
In Memoriam
FOURTH DIMENSION
Kiss Off!
EARLY DECAY
SURGEON GENERAL'S WARNING
AWARDS
STAINED TEETH
MOTION
BAD BREATH

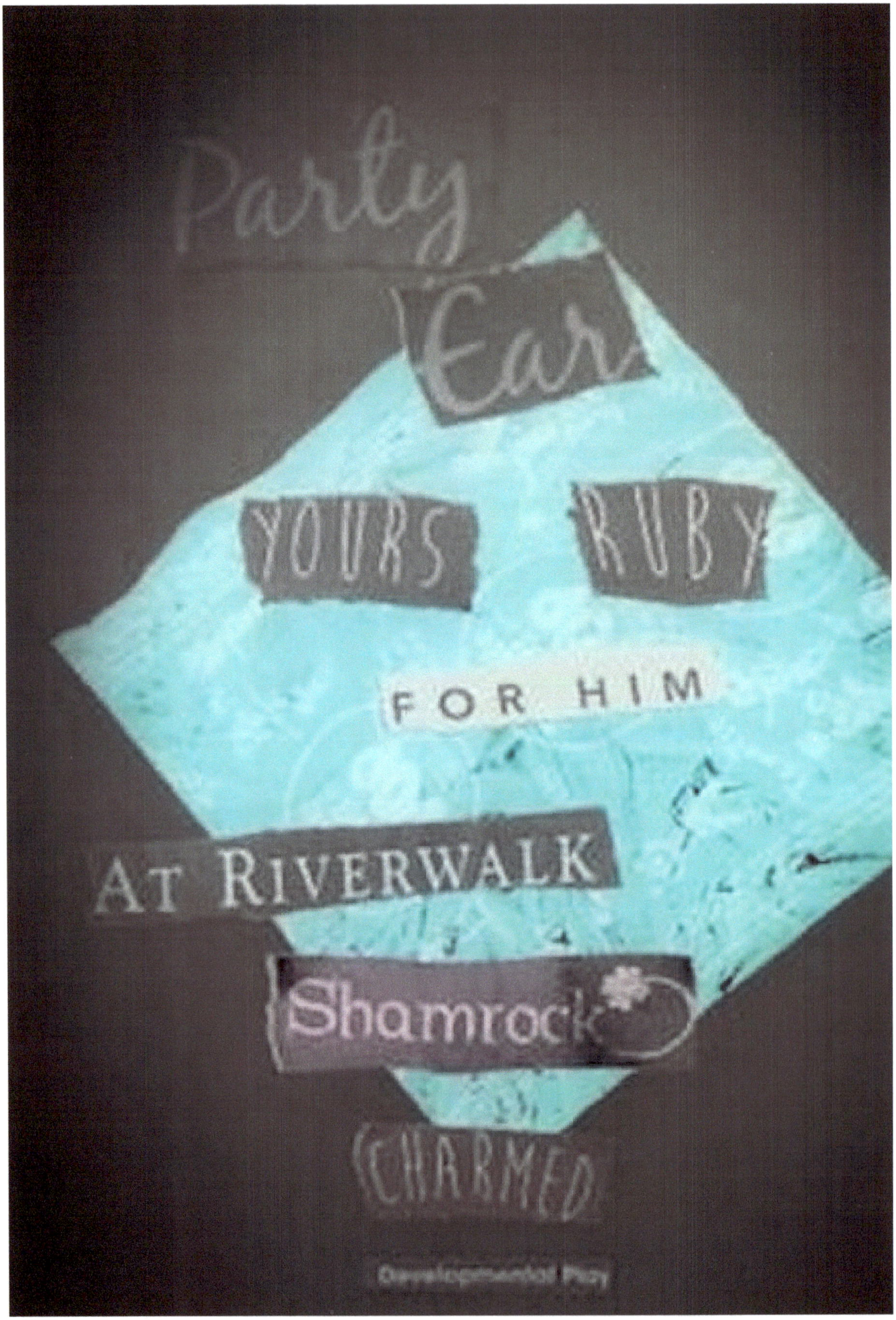
Party
Ear
YOURS RUBY
FOR HIM
AT RIVERWALK
Shamrock
CHARMED
Developmental Play

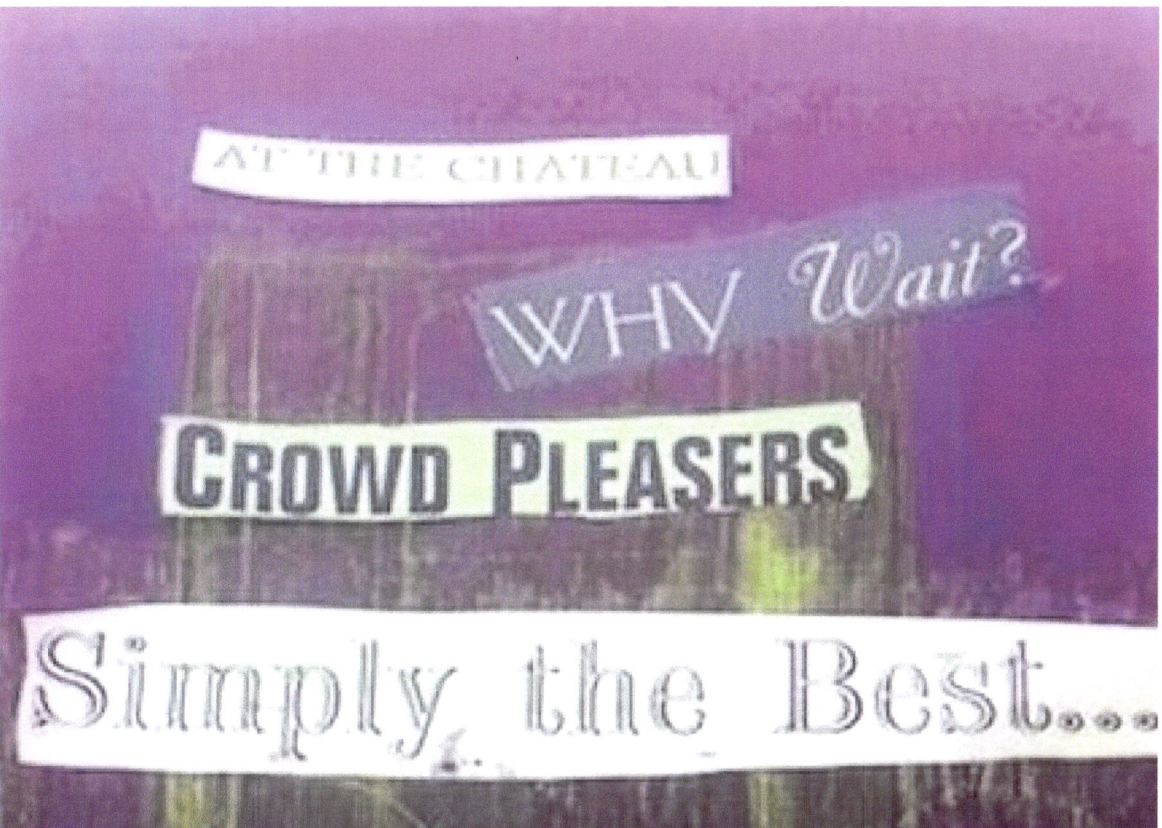

AT THE CHATEAU

WHY Wait?

CROWD PLEASERS

Simply the Best...

VISIONS OF FUTURE

Discover the Exceptional

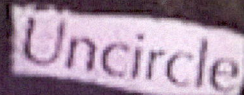

Uncircle

Yes, I know. They don't make an ounce of sense when you read them, but you can use what they *do* say to create possibilities. Let's look at the first picture: you see phrases such as "Puppets In Memoriam" or "Have you tried? Television" or "Surgeon General Warning Awards." Right there are three ideas that you can base your writing off of. When I read those phrases, I immediately thought of a cantankerous old lady with emphysema. The ventriloquist could state that her smoking is 'so bad she was nominated for a *Surgeon's General Warning Award*.' And when the ventriloquist suggests a new detoxing method for her, he can ask "Have you tried?" and she could interrupt him off with "Television, yeah done that *cough cough*"

Another Dadaist game is one called "Questions And Answers." How this works is with two players, each with an index card; one person writes five questions and the other writes five answers. This game can be reversed with "if" statements and "then" statements instead, but it's entirely up to you. But whatever you do, don't look at what the other person is writing. They will be read aloud together at the end.

The results you come up with can be hysterical. Here are a few results

that some friends and I compiled for fun:

What is free will? The answer to that question really depends on whether or

not you have the bends.

What is the best cure for a cold besides a hot toddy? My front tooth.

How do you get a snotty little prince to fall in love with you? Vampires bites.

If you ask (girl's name) out on a date; Then you might be a redneck

If (sports team) loses the next championship; Then all the beer in my fridge

will go flat.

If I were a superhero; Then there will never be a rainbow.

Now just imagine if that were ventriloquist dialogue. Dadaism is about

taking chances. One thing you could consider is playing a game like this

with a random audience member and then having your puppet read these

with you out loud. Guaranteed to get huge laughs.

MINIMALISM: This is a principle that can be applied to music as well.

It is when elements are pared down to the bare minimum. This is where the concept "less is more" stands to reason. As an art movement, it took place during the 1960s and featured works with geometric shapes and repetition. There was no ambiguity or element of surprise. This is one reason why these artists were recognized as "literalists." Now that definition makes it sound pretty boring, right? If this were applied to a character of yours, this would be a personality type called "deadpan." In other words, it describes a person that doesn't have much to say and appears dry and humorless. "Are they happy? Are they sad? No, they're just *there*." And guess what? That can be entertaining. I remember an episode of *Full House* back in the day when the character Kimmy Gibbler brought home a boyfriend named Dwayne. He never said anything except "whatever" and "I guess." He didn't present any facial expressions; he never laughed; never cried; never did a single thing except *that*. It was so minimal, yet so funny.

But minimalism can also be achieved in the simplicity of your character's look and feel. Take for instance Señor Wences using his hand as a puppet. His character "Johnny" wasn't a technically advanced figure in any way, but it didn't matter because he was very much alive and full of personality. And let's not forget Shari Lewis's Lamb Chop or Nina Conti's Monkey for that matter. Both very simple puppets, animation and personality to bring them to life. Take a look at the simplicity of the characters you see in the Pixar film *Toy Story*. Hardly any of the toys in that film have high tech features. Most are very basic, like a piggy bank or a potato head, but they were all very strong characters and essential to the story. Just remind yourself that if your figure actually *did* come to life, it wouldn't be like a pull string doll with only a limited number of catch phrases, it would have a mind of it's own and a big personality. But then again, Dwayne is proof that there are entertaining aspects that come along with having a more minimal personality. And even a minimal personality is better than no personality.

POP ART: This is an American movement from the 1950's that included imagery from newspapers or pop culture. One thing these artists also focused highly on was mass media. You may remember Andy Warhol's Campbell Soup Cans. If so, what did you notice about them? Did you notice a lot of repetition? This represented the fact that manufacturing produced popular items by the truck load and the advertisements for these products were ubiquitous. Pop Art is also a visual style, one that contains mostly primary colors and some of which have a "cartoony" style. Roy Lichtenstein is the best example of that. You notice in his works, he paints images of people in a comic book style and with random caption bubbles.

Key elements? **Mass media, pop culture,** and **cartoonish** features. In ventriloquism, this movement could certainly carry the greatest impact of all the ones listed. "Mass media" can lead to all sorts of humor, even pertaining to your figure *being* mass produced. Another thing this can play off of is politics. In a way, politicians are like manufactured robots and have as much interesting things to say as a "dummy" would. And let's not forget today's popular media; if being funny is your number one goal, pop culture always has a place in comedy.

Some of the best stand-up comedians out there base their humor off of what's in the media: ranging from popular movies; to popular music; to social media trends.

"Cartoony" characters are guaranteed to get the biggest laughs. What makes this strong is the fact that they enable an escape from reality for audience members. There's no limit on how colorful, how animated, and how loud they can be.

The best example of cartoony characters, in my opinion, is Jeff Dunham's Peanut. Peanut represents a lot of principles I've discussed with you thus far. For starters, he's cartoony. Secondly, he represents raw emotion with his "reactionary" humor. And third, he does embellish "less is more" physical attributes. He doesn't have the technical advancements of Jeff's other characters, but doesn't need them because he's loaded with a great big animated personality and that makes him such a strong character.

In the next two chapters, we will discuss principles as seen in Surrealism.

EXQUISITE CORPSE

In this chapter, we will explore one of the best known games in the art movement of Surrealism: *The Exquisite Corpse*. In many ways, Señor Wences was a Surrealist himself. His characters were so unconventional in the way he presented them. Take for instance Pedro in a box was literally a man's head in a box! Now who in the world would've thought of that? How do ideas like that even come to mind? Plus, he had so many skills such as plate spinning, juggling, drawing caricatures, etc. It was like ventriloquism was the envelope he could use to contain all of his talents.

Many recognize Surrealism as being art that best represents imagery in a dreamlike state. True, but it also represents images taken out of their original context for symbolic or experimental purposes. The Belgian Surrealist painter Rene Magritte did that very thing. One example of his work includes a painting of a living space with a green apple large enough to fill the entire room. Rene Magritte's playing with size and scale had a great influence on Pop Art, as you'll see all kinds of mass media pictures blown up into enormous sizes. Size, scale, unconventionality, and dreamlike imagery all play serious roles in a game of the Exquisite Corpse.

HOW TO PLAY: This game requires at least three players and three pieces of paper. Each paper must be folded into thirds. In the top section start by drawing a head with shoulders of some kind. Remember, it does not have to be a human head. In fact, it doesn't even have to be a head at all. I've seen people draw inanimate objects with eyes for that matter. The only rule is to make it seem like the top part of a unique creature.

Make sure you leave a few lines descending into the second folded section of the paper. Once you are done, fold your top section over so only the brief line work of the second section is showing. The next step is to pass to the person next to you so they can add to the middle section of the drawing without seeing what the top looks like. The same rule continues over and over again until an entire figure or "corpse" is completed.

What I have provided are examples of corpses that some theatre colleagues of mine and I collaborated on together:

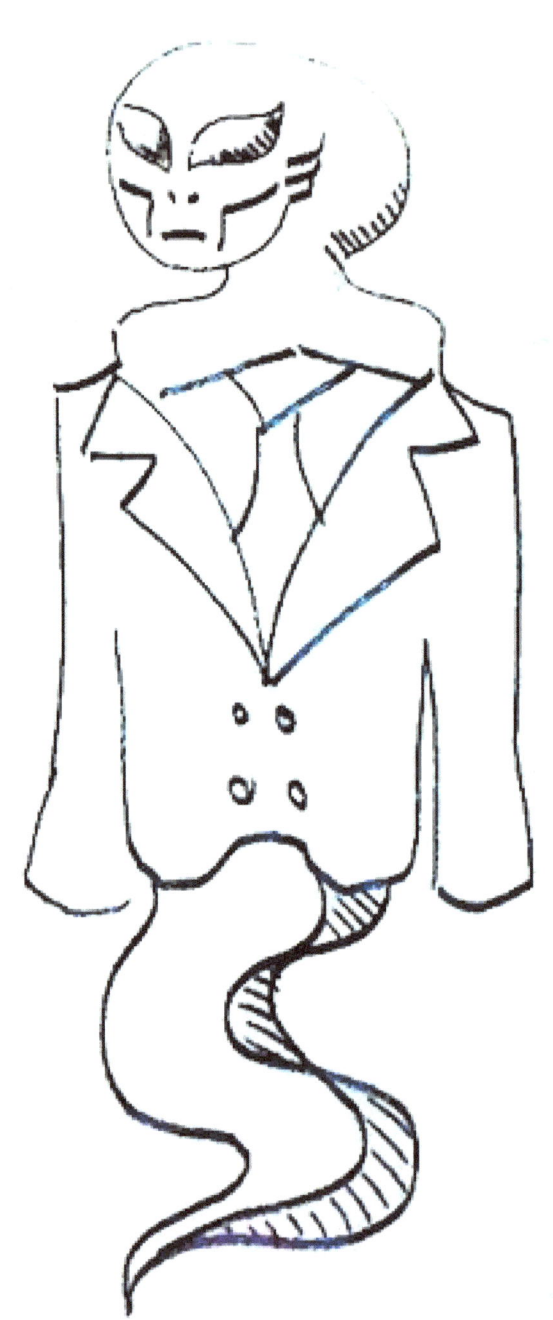

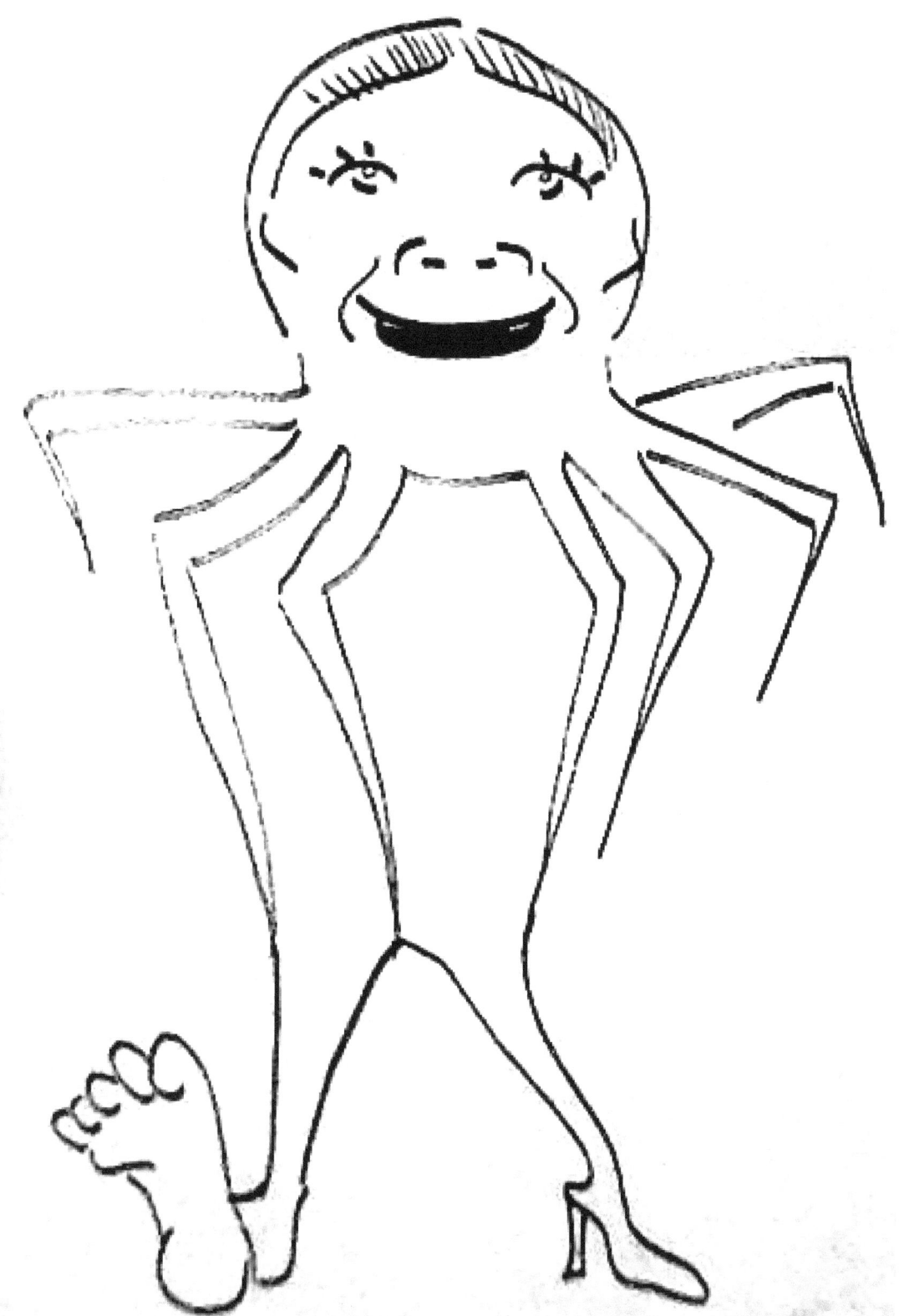

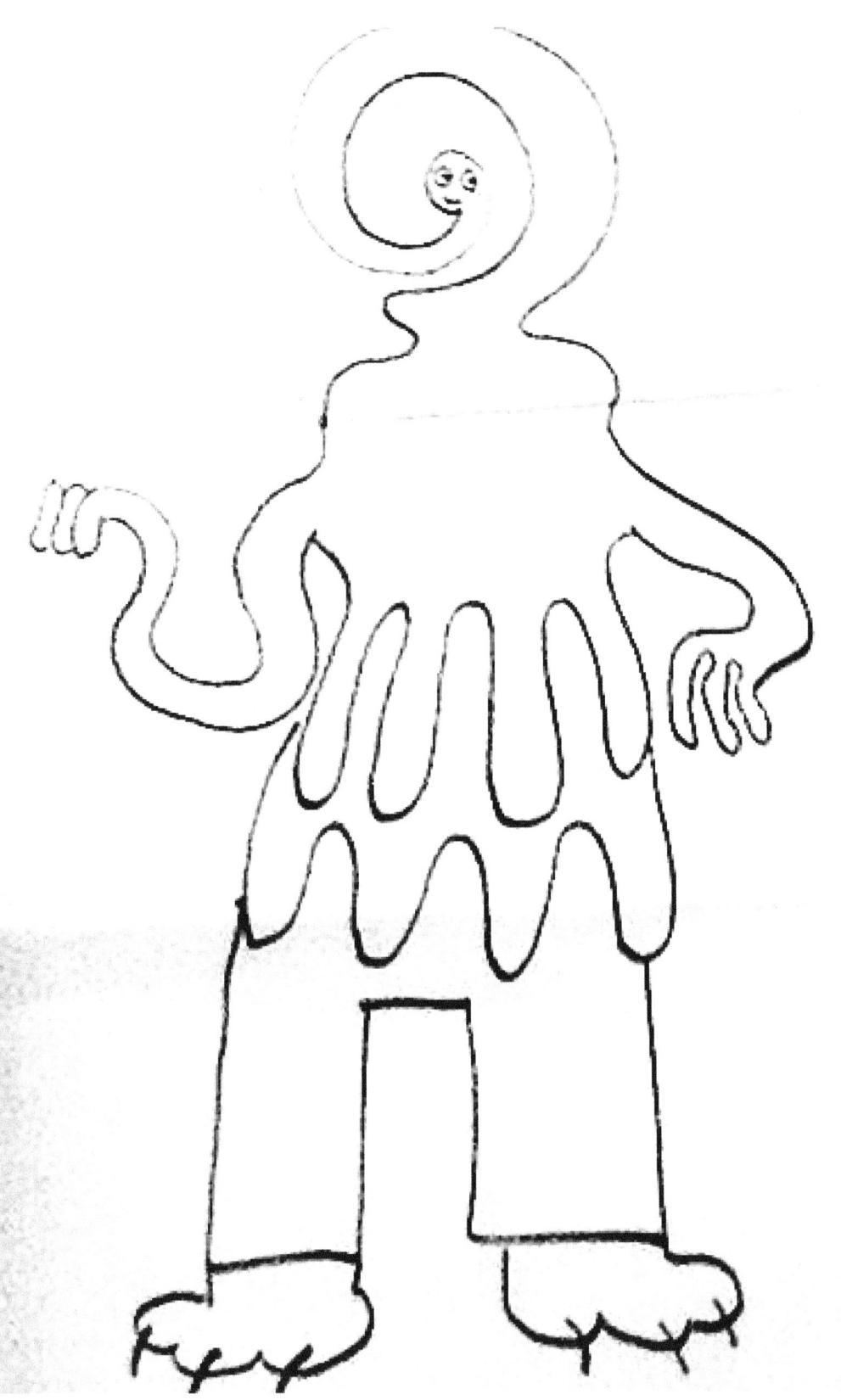

There you have it. Now what kind of an impact can this game have on ventriloquism? For starters, it can shape ideas for potential figures and it can also create possibilities for your writing. When putting together ideas for a figure using this technique, it is highly recommended to observe it carefully and make a list of ideas as to what it is that makes the image humorous. The vast majority of corpses you create will have a comical result. This is part of what makes "random humor" so strong.

The shock of an idea or image occurring is what random humor plays off of. Some good examples of successful "random" humor are seen in the animated videos of Don Hertzfeldt. One example is a video of a rugged character holding an enormous spoon over a cereal bowl. He keeps repeating that his spoon is too big. Out of the blue, a walking banana shows up and introduces himself. It's funny because it's something you least expect. That's what makes the Exquisite Corpse such an ideal strategy for critical thinking in this regard.

HYBRIDIZATION

In 1934, Rene Magritte created a work of art called "The Collective Invention." In this work, you see a mermaidesque figure, only different: instead of having a human top half and a fish bottom half, it's the other way around; a fish top half and the bottom half of a nude female. In art, the fusion of two beings or objects into one unique figure is called hybridization. This technique is one that Magritte has incorporated into multiple works over time.

Now imagine the character possibilities that can come from hybridization. Back to the cartoony side of things; in the mid 80's, there was a popular cartoon show that aired on CBS called *The Wuzzles*. In this show, each character was a hybrid of two different animals. For example, the character Rhinokey was part rhinoceros and part monkey; and the character Butterbear was part butterfly and part bear. These characters were brightly colored and inhabited a utopian landscape called the Isle of Wuz. Even the objects and architecture were hybrids of some kind (they lived in a castle-scraper and used a telephonograph). I loved this show growing up

because it was innovative, playful, and colorful. I can't even recall a single

cartoon that ever took on the same concept, but I could be wrong.

With hybridization, you're always going to get an original character.

The key is to bring together character types that are completely different and

find a common ground to bring them together. A rhinoceros and a monkey

are completely different species, yet they both live in tropical climates (there

you go, a common ground). And even if they could mate, their offspring

certainly wouldn't be the bright pink and yellow colors that Rhinokey was!

The goal of hybridization can also be achieved by fusing together *ideas*

instead of physical beings or objects. Take for instance characters from

Showbiz Pizza's animatronic band *The Rock-A-Fire Explosion*. In case you

weren't already aware, *Showbiz Pizza* was the original name of a children's

themed pizzeria before they were rebranded as *Chuck E. Cheese's* in 1992.

These are characters that hold a special sentiment from my childhood.

The characters were all animals taken out of their original context. One of these characters was a mouse in a cheerleading costume named Mitzi Mozzarella and another was a dog in a space suit named Dook: two highly unusual personas for their species. A mouse is one that most people would deem as discreet in fear of getting caught, not out in the open cheering and singing; and certainly not as large scale as she was.

One character that I found very ironic was "Beach Bear," a bear in swimming trunks surrounded by tropical plants and sky. The irony was the fact that he clearly resembled a polar bear! How does a polar bear end up in a pair of trunks while playing guitar on the beach? Why would *any* bear be seen at the beach let alone a polar bear? But hey, it's unique. My favorite character was Rolf de Wolf and his buddy Earle Schmerle. He was a tall wolf character that was *drumroll* a ventriloquist! Funny how he was so lighthearted and goofy instead of bloodthirsty and rabid.

Characters like these are bound to be conversation starters with your audience members and they will spark imagination for children and adults at all times. One of my characters is a yellow snail that wears a snappy suit, but yodels and sings country music. It started with the idea of giving him an energy drink to speed up and break into fast tempo songs like "The Auctioneer" by Leroy Van Dyke. I love playing with opposites and we all know a snail would be the last creature to have any kind of speedy nature. Eventually, I threw in a Southern accent and had him cultivate an "aw shucks" image. It ended up working really well for him. And to play on irony, I named him Salty. I often get asked "but doesn't salt kill snails?" and it immediately leads to a joke. My answer is the same every time: "Yes. But he doesn't know that, so don't tell him."

So here's the plan: on the next page, I have left a couple of tables for you when you are planning your character ideas. Think of the type of puppet you either do have, or plan to (you can list more than one). Make a list of adjectives that you wouldn't think to associate with this character until you find one that intrigues you. On the next page after, I included a venn diagram. In the diagram, map out what obscure similarities your figure and adjective have in common. Ask yourself how you can bring these opposing ideas together. Critical thinking is key.

ADJECTIVES	FIGURE(S)

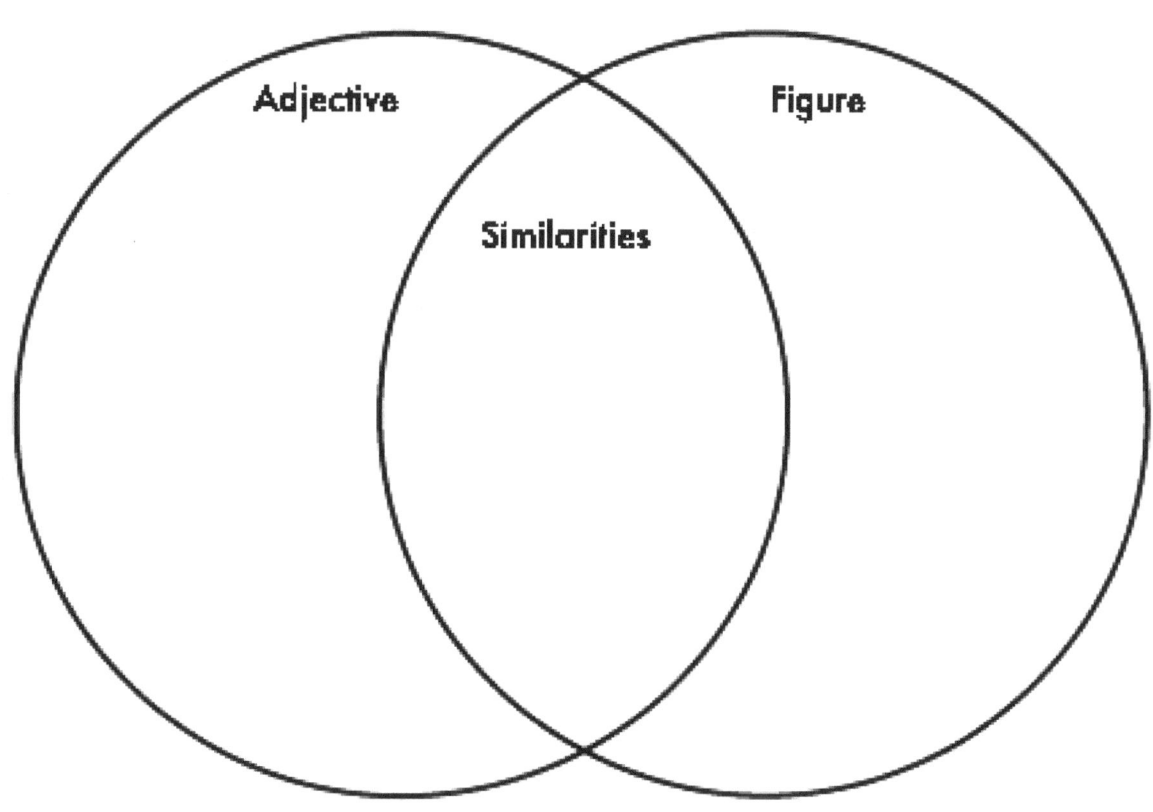

ADDITIONAL NOTES:

_____
_____
_____
_____
_____
_____
_____
_____
_____
_____

Once you feel you have achieved a starting point, the act writing can

begin. In the next chapter, we will explore the art and literary term Magic

Realism. This is one that plays on the use of exaggeration in your act.

MAGIC REALISM

Magic Realism is quite possibly my favorite art movement. It was most prominent in the 1920's-1940's and an artist that I am going share information about is easily my favorite painter of all time: Ivan Albright. He is a Chicago artist best known for his painting of Dorian Grey in the film adaption of Oscar Wilde's *The Picture of Dorian Grey* from 1945.

Magic Realism is what I like to refer to as a "tall tale" movement (I will explain that shortly). It depicts imagery of everyday reality with surreal undertones. In Ivan's paintings, he models the form and color schemes for a profound macabre effect. I like to think of him as the Godfather of Horror for that very reason. In his works, his color schemes include deteriorated shades of green, grey, and flesh tones. Sacks of drooping skin and bumpy textures are present in the reddened complexions of the people he paints, including his own self portraits. The subject matter is always standard, such as a woman seated or a wreath of flowers hung on the outside of a door. But what makes them powerful is not *what* these images are of, but *how* they are produced.

Exaggeration like this is key in famous tall tales. Take for instance the visual language in Stephen Vincent Benet's *The Devil & Daniel Webster*; the story of a farmer named Jabez Stone, from New Hampshire, who is plagued with bad luck, causing him to finally swear to sell his soul to the devil. Jabez is visited the next day by the devil himself, named "Mr. Scratch" who arranges such an offer. One description of the devil is "lantern-jawed." Read that adjective to yourself, what visuals come to mind? How could you take that and present it in a vent figure? One could go the literal route and construct a puppet from a lantern, or one could perhaps triple the size of the jawline and incorporate some kind of fire in the mouth.

Daniel Webster is one example of a tall tale (and in my opinion the greatest one). A tall tale has such highly unrealistic elements, but it's presented as if it were a true story. Some of these stories actually were based on real events, but the exaggerations create the fiction. For example, if a story's protagonist had large muscles, he wouldn't be described as "more muscular than the average man." Rather, the story would state that he "had biceps like two ten ton barrels." Language like this can create a type of humor bordering on the egotistical. Couldn't you see a body-builder puppet speaking fondly of himself with such dialogue? But remember, it doesn't have to be completely visual. It can simply be the writing. The character can be highly egotistical and delusional of himself and describes his capabilities with a God complex. Writing goes a long way in a single vent act.

If this type of writing or figure doesn't appeal to you, you can always incorporate tall tales into a ventriloquial story time. Your figure's reactions to such language can create humor and even interact with the audience. I have done a number of story times in my career and children absolutely love books that are attention grabbers; especially if your figure plays on these literary aspects. If a character in the book was described to have muscles like "ten ton barrels," you can count on a room full of kids yelling out "daaaaang!" This is a good opportunity for your puppet to establish a rapport with them. Hey, why not have the character yell "Daaaang" too? You could even have him try to compete with the characters in the books.

Figure: Oh yeah, well check out these muscles

Ventriloquist: Your arms are as skinny as my fingers.

Figure: So says you!

DECONSTRUCTION

Deconstruction art has multiple definitions. I'm going to share two types with you. The first example I am going to discuss is a Dadaist approach to Deconstruction: this functions by understanding how a work of art is created, followed by breaking it down into smaller parts (including breaking up the dialogue in bits), and then either cutting out or rearranging all the elements for a different kind of interpretation. I experimented with this when I collaborated on an experimental theatre project with colleagues from a Lawrence, KS community theatre company called EMU in 2012. This was arranged by the group deciding on a story to tell, one in which most people were already familiar with. The story we agreed on was *The Little Mermaid* by Hans Christian Anderson. It started with all of us reading the story in it's entirety and finding quotes from outside sources, including archives from publications of the Disney book. These pieces were then cut up and reassembled into a whole new piece.

A second way to deconstruct is to focus on a single idea and to stretch it out longer for an entire setting. A playwright who was known for having this kind of deconstructive style was Samuel Beckett. His plays all have a certain focus, but what makes them unique is their vagueness. Beckett also uses long and choppy dialogue. His characters' speeches are normally long in duration but if they are shorter, then they are spread out for longer periods of time with stage direction in between.

In our version of *The Little Mermaid,* we included a Beckett inspired piece. At the very beginning of the fairy tale itself, it is stated that each one of the mermaid sisters was privileged with the opportunity to visit the surface on their fifteenth birthday. Each one witnessed a completely different experience, but it didn't go into great length. In our Beckett piece, we closely examined each mermaid sister and presented each one with a lengthy monologue describing their experience in choppy, yet visually enticing dialogue. The stage set was empty. It wasn't presented with a beginning, middle, and end. Just the sisters and their experiences.

Who says a vent act has to be completely straight forward? It's valuable to give your audience something to remember, something that makes them think. The problem that most ventriloquists encounter is thinking too hard about being funny and not hard enough about being creative.

Jay Johnson's *Two & Only* slightly functions like a deconstructed work of art. He doesn't tell a classic story, but it's entirely based on his own career as a ventriloquist. He incorporates stand-up, childhood memories, and even educates the audience on the fundamentals of ventriloquism. It's absolutely brilliant! This work won him a Tony Award in 2007 for *Best Special Theatrical Event Show*. If you ever have the opportunity to hear Jay lecture, by all means do it.

Applying deconstruction to a vent act can function in multiple ways. You could use a famous story, a single idea, or you could use your own experiences. Just start by asking yourself what you would like to base your act off of and cut up the recipe. I have included a chart of what your process making should look like:

Story/ basis for act:	Strong/weak elements:
Creative writing methods to consider:	Sources to include:

Once you've broken down the recipe and included your own ingredients, you can arrange them however you like. This may function better as a group writing process for some, but it's not required.

Since I briefly mentioned breaking up dialogue, I'd like to end the chapter with this: a good way to experiment with chopping up dialogue for fun is to visit www.madglibs.com. On this website, you are presented with a large assortment of paragraphs such as personal letters, song lyrics, jingles, and so forth. Once a paragraph is chosen, you don't get to see what it says up front, but you will fill out an online form in which you will be asked to list random adjectives, nouns, verbs, and adverbs. These are used as replacement words for the paragraph. One example from the website is this Wal-Mart greeting:

Come shop at WALMART, where you`ll receive huge discounts on all of your favorite brand name items. Our friendly and helpful associates are there to guide you 24 hours a day. Here you will find low prices on the items you need, clothing for the moms, toys for the kids and all the latest electronics for the dads. So come on down to your locally owned WALMART *where the customers come first.*

Once I filled out the online form with random word types, this turned out to be my end result:

*Come **wheeze** at WALMART, where you`ll receive **gruesome** discounts on all of your favorite brand name **hooves**. Our **cuddly** and **hopping** associates are there to **shish-kabob** you **.02** hours a day. Here you will find **sterile** prices on the **stockings** you need. **girdles** for the moms, **childproof** **lighters** for the kids and all the latest electronics for the **Uncle-dads**. So come on down to your **skanky notorious** WALMART where the **pencil** **shavings** come first.*

Childproof lighters for the kids? That one gave me a huge chuckle because of the irony. The website is there for practice. This can also be sorted up in a game among friends. How that works is for you to write a paragraph and then underline certain words. Be sure to indicate whether they are nouns, verbs, adjectives, etc. If the first word you underlined is a noun, then have somebody in the room name a random noun; write it down next to the word. Keep this up with the rest of the underlined words until you have collected all of the ones you need: read aloud. Here is an example that I once created with my ex-roommate and her brother:

Original Paragraph: *The **sky** at **night** is full of **stars**. I love to **count** the stars as I **see** them one by one. The many **constellations** tell **powerful** stories. I wish I knew all the **stories.***

New Version: *The **girl** at **school** is full of **cats**. I love to **tickle** the stars as I **smell** them one by one. The many **lizards** tell **mawkish** stories. I wish I knew all the **deadbeats.***

Like the other games I've introduced to you in this book, this could also function as an interactive audience exercise. If you decide to use that, the only thing I would suggest is to stick with short and simple paragraphs like the ones above. Otherwise, it will take too long (remember, your audience has a limited attention span). If you perform nightclub shows, you can make this game as R-rated as you want. But if you are the type of vent who performs school assemblies, then this game can work as one that introduces children to Language Arts definitions. As I've stated before, with deconstruction, the possibilities are endless.

CUBISM

Cubism is one of the most influential art movements of the early 20th century. In Cubist work, objects are analyzed carefully and then broken up and reassembled; eliminating the possibility of one single focal point. This is a lot like Deconstruction, but not quite. While Deconstruction enables you to break down the story and retell by incorporating outside sources or eliminating parts, Cubism functions by keeping all of the same pieces, but reassembled into something completely different. Pablo Picasso is considered to be the Godfather of Cubism in fine art. A Cubist painting is most recognizable with it's use of geometric shapes as well as a composition that draws your eye to multiple view points. It contradicts the viewer's habitual response of staring straight to a central focal point.

Is this the way it is in ventriloquism? Having multiple focal points besides center stage? Not the last time I checked, but who says it can't happen? I could go on again about breaking down walls, but how exactly could we break those walls even further? Well, for one thing, I have seen some ventriloquists plant their figures in the audience and then bring them up to the front stage. The audience is a great place for the voice throwing illusion, no doubt. Does it have to be limited to just that? No. Let's explore ways to make the entire room a stage. I call this the 3 L's of Cubist Ventriloquism:

1. **Labyrinth:** Performing is not just about being on stage, anyone can do that. It's about *exploring the space;* making it your own. This is why theatre companies will warm their actors up with spatial exercises that enable such interpretive movements and vocal acoustics. Now, with what I am calling "Labyrinth Ventriloquism" you are exploring the space by constantly changing where you want your audience to focus on you, like following a big maze. This even gives them a chance to stand up and stretch in between acts. Let's face it, sitting in the same chair for long periods of time can be tiring and physically painful. In the end, they'll appreciate it (I hope). By switching your locations per act (but in the same room), you are creating a unique set of visual cues and surprising elements. I've seen famous singers make their live entrances on suspensions lowering from the rafters. Have you ever seen a vent do that? Yeah, me neither. This is also good for those

who perform strolling vent gigs. Constant movement and interaction with everyone that passes you (or the ones you pass) can bring out the best of your performing abilities up close. Children, in particular, love to meet eye to eye with your characters.

2. **Large Group Interaction:** Whenever someone raises their hand to ask questions, immediately the people in the room turn to face that person. Up close, personal interaction with your audience is not just for kids. Comedian Howie Mandel has been known to play tricks on his audience members during his standup. One example includes a time when a woman stood up to use the restroom and he then asked the remaining audience members to move two seats down so that she would be confused by the time she came back. It was a brilliant moment in comedy because suddenly his audience became cast members in his show. This was an opportunity for people to take their eyes (and bodies for that matter) elsewhere.

3. **Land Mine:** Remember the first time you visited a Haunted House and were startled by the many things that either shot at you or sprayed you from the last place you expected? I know I do. Now this is something that

could come in handy for ventriloquists who perform with a horror theme.

Horror and ventriloquism go hand-in-hand. With movies like *Dead Silence*,

Magic, and *Goosebumps*, it proves that ventriloquism can always have a

scare factor. You'll hear a lot of people say that the horror genre makes a

"mockery" of ventriloquists. It doesn't! It's just a separate genre. Horror is

an entertainment staple and that's never going to change. Now, with "land

mine ventriloquism," this is where surprise factors from your act can appear

quickly in various angles of the room, startling your audience as if they sat

close by a land mine. One example could be having a separate speaker in the

center of the room wired up so that you can increase the intensity of your

voice throwing illusion. It can be funny and scary, or maybe both.

I hope the ideas in this chapter and the previous ones enable you to

think critically and creatively about your act.

Dedicated to the younger generations of vents who are fighting for the future of ventriloquism. Keep doing what you're doing. Remember, there will be tough times, but these can lead to some of the greatest moments in your life. The quote "Ad Astra Per Aspera" on the Kansas flag is Latin for "To The Stars Through Difficulties." Remember that phrase when you encounter hardships along the way. It is the stars you aim for, after all.

-Rockwell

BIBLIOGRAPHY

Alden, Todd. *The Essential René Magritte*. New York: H.N. Abrams, 1999. Print

Albright, Ivan, and Michael Croydon. *Ivan Albright*. New York: Abbeville, 1978. Print.

Baker, Kenneth. *Minimalism: Art of Circumstance*. New York: Abbeville, 1988. Print.

Beckett, Samuel. *Collected Shorter Plays*. New York: Grove, 1984. Print.

Benét, Stephen Vincent, and Townsend Ludington. *The Devil and Daniel Webster and Other Writings*. New York: Penguin, 1999. Print

Brotchie, Alastair, and Mel Gooding. *Surrealist Games*. Boston: Shambhala Redstone Editions, 1993. Print.

Cox, Neil. *Cubism*. London: Phaidon, 2000. Print.

Elger, Dietmar, and Uta Grosenick. *Dadaism*. Koln: Taschen, 2004. Print

Hess, Barbara, and Uta Grosenick. *Abstract Expressionism*. Köln: Taschen, 2005. Print.

James, Jamie. *Pop Art*. London: Phaidon, 1996. Print.

Jay Johnson: The Two & Only!. Bryan Simon, Jay Johnson, 2014. DVD.

"The Rock-afire Explosion." *Wikipedia*. Wikimedia Foundation, n.d. Web. 27 Oct. 2016.

"The Wuzzles." *Wikipedia*. Wikimedia Foundation, n.d. Web. 27 Oct. 2016.

ACKNOWLEDGEMENTS

Special thanks to my parents for supporting me in all that I do and for putting up with me when I'm hard to be around. You've been kind, loving, generous, and loyal. Love you both unconditionally. God bless. Also, my brother Andy and sister Jenny for their kindness and generosity over the years. A special shout out to Gwethalyn Williams and everybody from EMU Theatre in Lawrence, KS. You have helped me discover who I am today.

Without these wonderful people in the vent community, none of this would be possible (no particular order):

Charles Prouty
Bob Rumba
Kenneth McGrath
Dan Horn
Tom Ladshaw
Jay Johnson
Terry Fator
Mark Wade
Nate Puppets
Vinnie Ewart
Ron Scherer
Matt Bailey
Christopher Ortiz
Jonelle Vandelft
Jeremy Lepak
Clair & Seth (don't ask me how to spell their last names)
Jim Barber
Brenda Hahn
Terry Eliason-Wells
Ian Varella
Daniel Clemente
Trish Dunn
Lori Bruner
Dana Barnum
Ed Casey
Meghan Casey
Adam De Fillippi

This list is of a few, but not limited to. If there's anyone I left out, I do apologize.

And lastly, I thank <u>YOU</u> the reader for taking the time to learn these new steps with me. I hope they become beneficial for you. Best of luck to you and your endeavors! 😃

www.ingramcontent.com/pod-product-compliance
Lightning Source LLC
Chambersburg PA
CBHW050801180526
45159CB00004B/1511